# EMBRACING FORGIVENESS

## *Barbara Cawthorne Crafton*
### *on What It Is and What It Isn't*

A 5-SESSION STUDY
BY BARBARA CAWTHORNE CRAFTON
WITH TIM SCORER

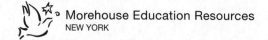
Morehouse Education Resources
NEW YORK

Editorial Offices: Morehouse Education Resources,
a division of Church Publishing Incorporated
Editorial Offices: 600 Grant Street, Suite 630, Denver, CO 80203
1-800-672-1789
*www.Cokesbury.com*

ISBN-13: 978-1-60674-198-6

# TABLE OF CONTENTS

# QUICK GUIDE TO THE HANDBOOK

## TEN things to know as you begin to work with this resource:

### 1. HANDBOOK + WORKBOOK

This handbook is a guide to the group process as well as a workbook for everyone in the group.

### 2. A FIVE-SESSION RESOURCE

Each of the five sessions presents a distinct topic for focused group study and conversation.

### 3. DVD-BASED RESOURCE

The teaching content in each session comes in the form of input by Barbara Crafton and response by members of a small group on a DVD recording of just over 30 minutes in length.

### 4. EVERYONE GETS EVERYTHING

This handbook addresses everyone in the group, not one group leader. There is no separate "Leader's Guide."

### 5. GROUP FACILITATION

The creators of this resource assume that someone will be designated as group facilitator for each session. You may choose the same person or a different person for each of the five sessions.

### 6. TIME FLEXIBILITY

Each of the five sessions is flexible and can be between one hour and two or more hours in length; however, if you intend to cover all the material presented, you will need the full two hours.

### 7. BUILD YOUR OWN SESSION

Prior to the session it is advisable for one or more members of the group to determine what to include in the group meeting time. The session outline presents options from which you can choose. They follow the flow of the DVD presentation, with the first options addressing Barbara Crafton's initial teaching in each session, and the later ones picking up on the issues raised by participants in the group with Barbara.

### 8. INSIDE EACH OPTION

Each option in a session features input from Barbara Crafton and the other members of the small group in the DVD, plus conversation openers to guide individual and group reflection.

### 9. BEFORE THE SESSION

Each session opens with five activities for participants to use as personal preparation prior to the session.

### 10. CLOSING AND BEYOND

Each session ends with an option that is a suggestion for ongoing personal engagement with the topic of the session. A closing prayer by Barbara Crafton is provided. Groups are encouraged to follow a prayer practice that reflects their own traditions and experience.

# BEYOND THE "QUICK GUIDE"

## Helpful information and guidance for anyone using this resource:

## 1. HANDBOOK + WORKBOOK

This handbook is a guide to the group process as well as a workbook for everyone in the group.
- We hope the handbook gives you all the information you need to feel confident in shaping the program to work for you and your fellow group members.
- The work space provided in the handbook encourages you...
  - — to respond to leading questions.
  - — to write or draw your own reflections.
  - — to note the helpful responses of other group members.

## 2. FIVE-SESSION RESOURCE

This resource presents Barbara Crafton's insights on Forgiveness, framed as five distinct topics of study:
1. Seventy Times Seven: Really?
2. You Have Heard It Said
3. Chipping Away
4. How to Start
5. Why Forgive?

## 3. DVD-BASED RESOURCE

The teaching content in each session comes in the form of input by Barbara Crafton and response by members of a small group; just over 30 minutes in length.

Barbara Crafton's focused and engaging presentations stimulate thoughtful and heartfelt conversation among her listeners.

The edited conversations present group sharing that builds on Barbara's initial teaching. They are intended to present to you a model of small group interaction that is personal, respectful and engaged.

You will notice that the participants in the DVD group also become our teachers. In many cases, quotes from the group members enrich the teaching component of this resource. This will also happen in your group—you will become teachers for one another.

We hope that the DVD presentations spark conversations about those things that matter most to those who are striving to understand the dynamics of forgiveness and the ways that our experience of Sacred Presence supports and inspires forgiveness in our lives.

## 4. EVERYONE GETS EVERYTHING

The handbook addresses everyone in the group, not one group leader. There is no separate "Leader's Guide."

Unlike many small group resources, this one makes no distinction between material for the group facilitator and for the participants. Everyone has it all! We believe this empowers you and your fellow group members to share creatively in the leadership.

## 5. GROUP FACILITATION

We designed this for you to designate a group facilitator for each session. It does not have to be the same person for all five sessions, because everyone has all the material. It is, however, essential that you and the other group members are clear about who is facilitating each session. One or two people still have to be responsible for these kinds of things:

- making arrangements for the meeting space (see notes on Meeting Space, p. 8 )
- setting up the space to be conducive to conversations in a diverse small group community
- creating and leading an opening to the session (see notes on Opening, p. 8 )
- helping the group decide on which elements of the guide to focus on in that session
- facilitating the group conversation for that session
- keeping track of the time
- calling the group members to attend to the standards established for the group life (see notes on Group Standards, p. 8)
- creating space in the conversation for all to participate

- keeping the conversation moving along so that the group covers all that it set out to do
- ensuring that time is taken for a satisfying closing to the session
- making sure that everyone is clear about date, location and focus for the next session
- following up with people who missed the session

## 6. TIME FLEXIBILITY

Each of the five sessions is flexible and can be between one hour and two or more hours in length; however, if you intend to cover all the material presented, you will need the full two hours.

We designed this resource for your group to tailor it to fit the space available in the life of the congregation or community using it. That might be Sunday morning for an hour before or after worship, two hours on a weekday evening, or 90 minutes on a weekday morning.

Some groups might decide to spend two sessions on one of the five major topics. There's enough material in each of the five outlines to do that. Rushing to get through more than the time comfortably allows, results in people not having the opportunity to speak about the things that matter to them.

## 7. BUILD YOUR OWN SESSION

Prior to the session it is advisable for one or more members of the group to determine what to include in the group meeting time. The session outline presents options from which you can choose.

- One or two people might take on the responsibility of shaping the session based on what they think will appeal to the group members. This responsibility could be shared from week to week.
- The group might take time at the end of one session to look ahead and decide on what they will cover in the next session. In the interest of time, it might be best to assign this planning to a couple of members of the group.
- You might decide to do your personal preparation for the session (the five activities in "Before the Session"), and when everyone comes together for the session, proceed on the basis of what topics interested people the most.

## 8. INSIDE EACH OPTION

Each segment in a session features a mix of input from Barbara Crafton and the other members of the small group in the video, plus questions for discussion or other creative activities to guide individual and group reflection.

You will recognize that the activities and topics in the study guide emerge both from the structured teaching of Barbara Crafton as well as the informal and spontaneous conversation of the group members. This parallels the process of your group, which will be initially led by the content of the DVD and the study guide, but then branch off in directions that emerge spontaneously from the particular life of your group.

## 9. BEFORE THE SESSION

Each session opens with five activities for participants to use as personal preparation prior to the session.

We intend these activities to open in you some aspect of the topic being considered in the upcoming session. This may lead you to feel more confident when addressing the issue in the group.

Sometimes these questions are the same as ones raised in the context of the session. They offer the opportunity for you to do some personal reflection both before and/or after engaging in the group conversation on that topic.

## 10. CLOSING AND BEYOND

Each session has a *final reflective option* for participants to take from the session and use as an extension of their learning. These offer a disciplined way for each participant to continue to harvest the riches of the group conversation.

A *closing prayer* is provided at the end of each session. Groups are encouraged to follow a prayer practice that reflects their own traditions and experience.

Another aspect of closing is *evaluation*. This is not included in an intentional way in the design of the sessions; however, evaluation is such a natural and satisfying thing to do that it could be included as part of the discipline of closing each session. It's as simple as taking time to respond to these questions:

- What insights am I taking from this session?
- What contributed to my learning?
- What will I do differently as a result of my being here today?

## 1. Meeting Space

- Take time to prepare the space for the group. When people come into a space that has been prepared for them, they trust the hospitality, resulting in a willingness to bring the fullness of them into the conversation. Something as simple as playing recorded music as people arrive will contribute to this sense of "a space prepared for you."
- Think about how the space will encourage a spirit of reverence, intimacy and care. Will there be a table in the center of the circle where a candle can be lit each time the group meets? Is there room for other symbols that emerge from the group's life?

## 2. Opening

- In the opening session, take time to go around the circle and introduce yourselves in some way.
- Every time a group comes together again, it takes each member time to feel fully included. Some take longer than others. An important function of facilitation is to help this happen with ease, so people find themselves participating fully in the conversation as soon as possible. We designed these sessions with this in mind. Encouraging people to share in the activity proposed under *Group Life* is one way of supporting that feeling of inclusion.
- The ritual of opening might include the lighting of a candle, an opening prayer, the singing of a hymn where appropriate, and the naming of each person present.

## 3. Group Standards

- There are basic standards in the life of a group that are helpful to name when a new group begins. Once they are named, you can always come back to them as a point of reference if necessary. Here are two basics:
  - Everything that is said in this group remains in the group. *(confidentiality)*
  - We will begin and end at the time agreed. *(punctuality)*
- Are there any others that you need to name as you begin? Sometimes standards emerge from the life of the group and need to be named when they become evident, otherwise they are just assumed.

The lack of forgiveness that we experience is really an opportunity for us to come closer to God [as we ask] for help. It makes us better than we were.

—Barbara Cawthorne Crafton

# SESSION | 1

## SEVENTY TIMES SEVEN: REALLY?

### BEFORE THE SESSION

Many participants like to come to the group conversation after considering individually some of the issues that will be raised. The following five reflective activities are intended to open your mind, memories and emotions regarding some aspects of this session's topic. Use the space provided here to note your reflections.

1. The title for this session comes from Matthew 18:21-22. Before coming to the session and listening to Barbara's reflection on these two verses, take your own time to sit with them and hear what there is for you in Peter's question and Jesus' response: *At that point Peter got up the nerve to ask, "Master, how many times do I forgive a brother or sister who hurts me? Seven?" Jesus replied, "Seven! Hardly. Try seventy times seven.*

2. Go to the first option, *Plumbing Our Own Experience* (p. 15) and, in anticipation of the group conversation in which you will participate, give yourself time to reflect on the five quotes from Barbara Crafton and the five questions.

3. Take time for some life review, remembering times when you learned most about forgiveness. What wisdom do you carry with you today as a result of those episodes in your life? Who taught you about forgiveness?

4. Take time to think about the theme of forgiveness in your life just now. These questions may help you in your reflection: *Who is waiting for your forgiveness? Whose forgiveness are you aware of desiring? What relationships have been changed as a result of acts of forgiveness?*

5. What questions about forgiveness do you hope to have addressed in the course of this five-part series? Note those here for future reference.

The theme of this series is "Embracing Forgiveness." You have come together as a group, ready to uncover some responses to this question: What is forgiveness, and what is it not?

If this is a new group, meeting for the first time, take a few minutes to introduce yourselves in two ways:
• by telling your name
• by telling one thing that attracted you to participate in this program

In February of 2014, another group met in New York City, to learn with Barbara Crafton and to grapple with the same issues that are on your agenda for these five sessions.

Moving from left to right as you will see them on the screen, they are Tim Scorer (moderator and author of this study guide), Ralph, Ryan, Patrice, Tapua, George, Toni and Barbara Crafton. You won't hear from each person in every session, but over the course of five sessions you will hear contributions from all six participants in the group.

Before selecting from the options that follow as a guide and catalyst for conversation, together watch *the entire portion of the DVD for Session 1.*

## OPTION 1: PLUMBING OUR OWN EXPERIENCE

If you have more than eight people in your group, conduct the following conversation in pairs or groups of three. Having people in twos or threes at this point in the life of the group helps people to feel included, especially those for whom speaking in a larger group is a challenge.

Barbara states:

> *Everybody has something about forgiveness. There's somebody [who] did something terrible you can't get past, or maybe you did something you can't forgive yourself for, or [there's] someone else [who] can't forgive you.*

What is the first thing that comes to mind for you in this matter of forgiveness? What personal involvement in forgiving is still unfinished for you?

Barbara explains:

> *This idea of "forgiving as we have been forgiven"—maybe what it's saying is if you forgive, you will know what it is to be forgiven, and if you don't forgive, you won't be able to accept this gift. "It's not that I (God) am not giving it to you—I (God) am giving it to you all the time—it's that you won't be able to accept it."*

When have you experienced the power of forgiveness in the way that Barbara is describing? When have you received the gift of this reciprocal relationship between forgiving and being forgiven?

Barbara suggests:

*What makes forgiveness so impossible for us is the way anger functions in us over time. It latches on. It lands in the heart and makes like a tumor there. Over time it makes its own blood supply and pretty soon it can't be removed. It's gotten too deep; it's become a part of you and you feel as if you'd die. There are tumors like that; there are inoperable tumors you can't excise because you'd kill the patient. Anger, the holding of a grudge, the lack of forgiveness is a tumor—a growth in the spiritual body.*

When have you experienced the persistent presence of anger as a kind of tumor that makes it increasingly difficult to move to forgiveness?

Barbara assures us:

*I can't do much about what happened in the past, but I have a lot to say about who I'm going to be now and who I'm going to walk with. It's hard for us to choose life sometimes, but we can still make that choice and we have help. We don't have to do it all alone.*

What's one choice you are sitting with right now that could make a difference about how you move forward with life and with the possibility of grace? How will you remember that you are not alone?

Barbara tells us:

*The lack of forgiveness that we experience is really an opportunity for us to come closer to God in asking for help. It makes us better than we were. That's paradoxical. "You mean this thing that I had, this sin of mine that I couldn't forgive or wouldn't forgive or that I could not get free from—my own shame— that thing is a means of grace?" Why, yes.*

When have you experienced the grace of God as a gift of one of these situations that seemed to be completely lacking in grace?

# OPTION 2: WE HAVE OPTIONS

*At that point Peter got up the nerve to ask, "Master, how many times do I forgive a brother or sister who hurts me? Seven?" Jesus replied, "Seven! Hardly. Try seventy times seven."*
(Matthew 18:21-22, *The Message*)

At the beginning of the DVD, Barbara names the Christian challenge in this way:

*I guess if I can't forgive seventy times seven, I can't be a good Christian. I'm just not the right kind of person. It feels like a ticket to Jesus' love that I can't afford. If I have to be forgiving, then I guess I can't come to the party.*

Patrice opens the conversation with her reflections about the power there is in choosing the gift of forgiveness for ourselves and for each other: "Each day we can choose to make forgiveness a way of life."

Barbara responds that our power to choose can be impaired, and we don't realize the power we actually have: "We think we have to feel the way we feel because we've always felt that way." She offers the perspective we share as people of the Way of Jesus: "Jesus offers us options. He often flies in the face of what everybody else thinks is true and encourages people to question what is the commonly held wisdom. We carry things around and burden ourselves with them because we don't really know we can put them down."

Jesus says, in Matthew 11:28-30 *(NRSV)*:

*Come to me, all you that are weary and are carrying heavy burdens, and I will give you rest. Take my yoke upon you, and learn from me; for I am gentle and humble in heart, and you will find rest for your souls. For my yoke is easy, and my burden is light.*

1. When have you ever felt like these words of Jesus touched you and made a real difference?

2. What makes it challenging sometimes for you to make forgiveness a way of life?

## OPTION 3: FREEING UP SPACE

Ralph opens us into a consideration of the results of being able to forgive ourselves:

> *When things turned around for me, the hardest thing to do was to forgive myself. Eventually, as time went on, I let it go. Everybody forgave me. It took a long time. Once you do it—forgive yourself—it's like dropping a big weight.*

Barbara draws our attention to the heart space as she says:

> *It frees up a lot of space here that you could use for something else.*

1. When have you had that experience of space being opened up as a result of forgiving or being forgiven? Try talking about it from the perspective of your heart and your body, rather than your head.

2. What space in your body today is taken up with something that you would be relieved to release? that would allow space for something good to come in? How might you go about that?

# OPTION 4: JUSTICE AND FORGIVENESS

George brings to the conversation what he sees as "the opposing values" of forgiveness and justice:

> *My desire to see the right done by me or someone else is a strong demand. It's hard for me to imagine forgiveness that doesn't involve the sacrifice of justice. If I make my demand for justice an absolute, then life doesn't work. It's not easy to let go if some injustice has been done either to me or to someone else.*

Barbara opens a number of windows for us to examine this complex issue. You have heard her speaking on the DVD. Here are two key points for your consideration:

> *When we talk about forgiveness it might sound as if we are saying, "Well, you don't have to pay the consequences. It's all okay." But forgiveness has nothing to do with acquittal. Forgiveness is not exoneration.*

> *Society has a duty to make justice as present in its midst as it can. Forgiving does not absolve us of that duty. It's part of life together. We often think that when we say "I forgive you" that I'm saying 'That's okay." Okay has nothing to do with forgiveness. You don't have to forgive things that are okay. Forgiveness admits the person you are forgiving—maybe you—back into the human race. But as a member of the human race you may still have a debt to pay.*

1. When have you lived this tension between justice and forgiveness? What did you learn?

2. Where do you see this dance of justice and forgiveness being lived out in your community? What processes and practices exist to ensure that both justice and forgiveness are satisfied?

George returns with another related question:

*Is what we're leaning toward here that the grace of forgiveness is what ultimately will give us the ability to fight for justice? that forgiven, we can fight for justice?*

This provides Barbara with an opportunity to speak about the difference between the Biblical concept of justice and the classical one. Here are some of her key points:

*Our "classical" figure for justice is a lady with a blindfold holding a scale that is precarious in its balance. In this classical image, justice is precarious. It's which one is going to win: good or bad?*

*Hebrew culture rather sees justice not as a mutual restraint of evil but as a positive action of a righteous God who fights for you. The God who is actively seeking righteousness on the side of the people of God is different from a blindfolded figure holding a precarious scale.*

*The righteousness of God pushes beyond "an eye for an eye and a tooth for a tooth." "I'm not going to hurt you anymore than you hurt me" is a balance, but is it necessarily a loving thing?*

*There is an energetic pursuit of the good [that] is the conviction that the good of the other is as good as my good and that I should be passionate in the pursuit of it.*

*There's a passion in our pursuit of justice that is missing in what we have received from the classical world. Perhaps we have confused what is just with what is legal?*

1. What personal and communal stories do you have which illustrate this Biblical tradition of justice that takes us beyond the balancing act of the classical tradition?

2. How does this Biblical approach to justice affect the way we live forgiveness?

# OPTION 5: CLOSING PRAYER

Most loving God,
you know that we have a hard time forgiving even once.
Help us to hear Jesus' challenge to forgive,
not as a judgment on our weakness
but as an invitation to put our trust in you
to accomplish in us what we cannot accomplish in ourselves.
This we ask in the name of our Savior Jesus Christ.
*Amen.*

*Barbara Cawthorne Crafton, 2014*

# OPTION 6: PERSONAL REFLECTION

### (for use following the session)

Following the session you will continue to think about issues raised both on the DVD and in your small group. This suggestion for journaling is offered to support you in continuing your reflection beyond the session time.

1. You may not have had time to complete all the options in the group study time. As you have time, take the opportunity for personal reflection on the ones that you missed, or the ones that were really engaging and to which you now want to return on your own.

2. The subject matter and process of this session is very personal and might have opened a place of vulnerability in you. How will you care for yourself?
   - You might choose to seek out another member of the group for further conversation.
   - You might feel that you are ready to approach someone with whom you have unfinished business in the matter of forgiving and being forgiven.
   - You might want to spend time with a person skilled in pastoral care, counseling, or spiritual direction to address some of the issues that have arisen for you.
   - You might use a journal or other expressive media to enable you to explore further the relational issues that came up in the course of this session.

3. Having met Barbara Cawthorne Crafton on DVD, you might be curious to know more about her ministry and to subscribe to *The Almost Daily eMos*. Go to *http://www.geraniumfarm.org/home.cfm* for more information on Barbara and The Geranium Farm.

What will lead you to forgiveness is your will. I can't make myself stop hurting, but I can make myself take a step forward.

—Barbara Cawthorne Crafton

# SESSION | 2

## You Have Heard it Said...

### BEFORE THE SESSION

Many participants like to come to the group conversation after considering individually some of the issues that will be raised. The following five reflective activities are intended to open your mind, memories and emotions regarding some aspects of this session's topic. Use the space provided here to note your reflections.

1. In anticipation of the group discussion, review the six items in the first option, *You Have Heard It Said…But I Say To You…* (p. 29) where Barbara refutes six commonly held "truths" about forgiveness. There will be an opportunity in the group conversation to speak about the way that one of these six intersects with your own life experience.

2. In the second option, *Forgiveness as Process* (p. 31), there is an emphasis on forgiveness as a process rather than a discrete moment. Quietly recall times in your life when you have worked through a process of forgiveness that over time has led to a change of relationship—perhaps restoration, perhaps not.

3. Is there someone close by with whom you have lived through a process of forgiveness or being forgiven? Perhaps it would be fruitful to talk with this person about that shared experience. You might learn more about the deeper wisdom of forgiveness through reflection with someone who, like you, was intimately involved in it.

4. Barbara makes reference to the way in which Jesus took the commonly held cultural and religious truisms of his time and turned them upside down. Read Matthew 5, where you will find a portion of the Sermon on the Mount where Jesus uses that verbal structure ("You have heard that it was said…but I say to you.") in his teaching.

5. This week, notice what practices you have—some of which you may be unaware of—that support your intention to engage in forgiveness in helpful and life-affirming ways.

The theme of this series is "Embracing Forgiveness." You have come together as a group, ready to uncover some responses to these questions: *What is forgiveness? What is it not?*

As you come together, you all bring thoughts about forgiveness that are rooted in your life experience. Go around the circle and remind people of your name, then say one thing to complete this statement, "Forgiveness is _____."

At the end of the session, take note of any way that this thing you said about forgiveness has changed as a result of the input of the session.

Before selecting from the options that follow as a guide and catalyst for conversation, together watch the *entire portion of the DVD for Session 2*.

## OPTION 1: YOU HAVE HEARD IT SAID... BUT I SAY TO YOU...

One of the reasons that we have a hard time with forgiveness is that we hold incorrect ideas about what it is. Perhaps we are trying to do things in forgiveness that are not life-giving, edifying and useful.

Here is a review of six things that Barbara refutes as characteristics of forgiveness. For each one, there is a quote or two from Barbara to remind you of the fullness of her teaching on that matter.

You have heard it said that to forgive is to forget, but I say to you *forgiveness is not forgetting*.

> *People don't forget important chapters in their lives. Forgiveness does not erase history.*

> *Your history has happened and it deserves to be honoured. If it's not honoured it's liable to be repeated.*

You have heard it said that to forgive is to acquit, but I say to you *forgiveness is not acquittal or exoneration*.

> *We still have to pay the price for what we do. If someone is acquitted it means they didn't do anything.*

> *We only forgive those who are guilty of something.*

You have heard it said that to forgive is to pardon, but I say to you *forgiveness is not pardon*.

> *Even when forgiven, you may still have to pay for what you did.*

> *When you are pardoned, you don't have consequences.*

You have heard it said that forgiveness is a matter of degree, but I say to you *forgiveness is not a matter of degree*.

> *We have confused our feeling of horror at the crime with the capacity or lack of capacity to forgive. Even one death is too much. It's difficult for us because of the horror we feel for large and heinous crimes.*

> *We cannot say that the power of God is not greater than these things.*

> *It might take us a while to wrap our minds around this one; and longer to wrap our hearts around it.*

> *"Okay" has nothing to do with anything when we're talking about forgiveness.*

You have heard it said that forgiveness is led by feeling, but I say to you *forgiveness is not feeling.*

> *If forgiveness is a feeling and if somehow, in order to forgive, I have to develop warm fuzzy feelings about someone who did something horrible to me; or, with regard to my own shame, if somehow I have to develop feelings of being welcomed and loved before I can be forgiven—feelings can't lead me to that state.*

You have heard it said that forgiveness is all about the past, but I say to you *forgiveness is not about the past.*

> *Forgiveness is about the present and the future. Who do I want my future to belong to: the guy who hurt me in 1998 or me and God? I want to live my life with God. I don't want to give it to anybody else. I want my present to be mine. I want my future to be mine.*

As you listened to Barbara teaching about *what forgiveness is not*, where did you find her teaching intersecting with your lived experience? Which of these six "nots" has the most energy for you as you consider this matter of forgiveness? Share stories and insights in twos, threes or small group, as time allows.

# OPTION 2: FORGIVENESS AS PROCESS

In the midst of talking about what forgiveness is not, Barbara offers a helpful reflection on forgiveness as a process:

There's a trinity of the human being:
we are reason—we are feeling—we are will.
We are not any one of these three things exclusively.
All three are present in us, or we are not human.
No one of these three can lead all the time.
They each have functions.
We have to balance them.

In the project of forgiveness,
feelings aren't going to lead you there.
You might be too mad or too hurt.
But feelings can follow.
What will lead you to forgiveness is your will.
I can't make myself not hurt,
but I can make myself take a step forward.
If I can say, "I don't forgive him.
I don't even want to forgive him,
but I want to want to forgive;
I want to be different,"
then we've taken the first step.
We haven't taken the last;
forgiveness is a process, not a moment.

If you can say,
"Yes, I've begun the process of forgiving.
I haven't finished.
It might take a whole life time to finish it,
but I have begun here,
so I can answer yes."
My will has begun to lead me in a direction
that my feelings never could.
If I can take a small step,
God will bless that step and will increase it.
It is a theological decision.

1. Tell the story of a time when you experienced forgiveness as process, not as a moment.

2. Are there relationships in your life right now where you could make an act of will that would make a difference in the process of forgiveness?

# OPTION 3: AFTER THE FORGIVING

Tapua notes that even when there has been an act of forgiveness, not everything changes. The other person may still be difficult to deal with. They may not even accept your forgiveness if you have been the one forgiving. "It seems like there's a lot more work to be done in the rebuilding of the relationship even after you forgive."

Barbara catches the spirit of Tapua's comments with this: "It only makes it possible to have a relationship. It doesn't make it easy."

And Patrice offers the perspective that the first step of forgiveness is like a gift offered: "I can decide with what mindset I move into my future, what attitude toward life, toward the offender and toward myself."

"…and with help," adds Barbara. "I'm not strong enough to do this on my own. We have a power greater than ourselves that can help us do it."

1. What have you learned from experience about what comes after the act of forgiveness?

2. When have you experienced God's help and presence in these relational challenges as a power that makes it possible for you to do what you could not do alone?

# OPTION 4: PRACTICE, PRACTICE, PRACTICE

Toni offers reflection on the importance of practice in the forgiveness process:

> *How do you get to Carnegie Hall? Practice, practice, practice.*
>
> *How to you get to forgiveness? Practice, practice, practice.*
>
> *I'm always practicing whether or not I've got there. I practice by holding the person I want to forgive—just holding their name, just saying their name. It's something real I can do as I work through it.*

What practices have supported your intention to enter and move along the path of forgiveness?

# OPTION 5: GETTING TO WHAT'S POSSIBLE AND SAFE

Barbara brings sobering reflection as she speaks of the limits of restoration of relationship through forgiveness:

> *We think that forgiveness will mean the restoration of presence—that we can be together again. That's the dream—that forgiveness will bring community. It may not.*

> *That's painful because we all would wish it would be magical and if I forgive you, it would mean now that we could begin a life together such as we wanted. It may not be; but it can be a life, nonetheless, in which you both live in the world and you both are here and both are safe.*

You have heard Barbara speak on the DVD about this matter of limits in the restoration of relationship after forgiveness has been granted and, sometimes, received. What real situations come to mind for you in this matter of restoration's *limits*? Where have you seen instances of people arriving at a kind of safe and settled place that falls short of what they might have wished for? What makes it possible for them to live content in that place?

# OPTION 6: CLOSING PRAYER

Lord Jesus, our teacher and our guide,
give us wisdom and discernment
to regard what we have been taught throughout our lives
with a fresh pair of eyes and an open mind,
and help us never to forget
that we serve a God whose love far exceeds any other.
With the Father and the Holy Spirit, you reign in our hearts,
Lord Christ,
*Amen.*

*Barbara Cawthorne Crafton, 2014*

# OPTION 6: PERSONAL REFLECTION

**(for use following the session)**

Following the session you will continue to think about issues raised both on the DVD and in your small group. This suggestion for journaling is offered to support you in continuing your reflection beyond the session time.

1. You may not have had time to complete all the options in the group study time. As you have time, take the opportunity for personal reflection on the ones that you missed, or the ones that were really engaging and to which you now want to return on your own.

2. Take time to reflect (and perhaps journal) on how the input and conversation has changed your attitude toward forgiveness. *You had heard it said… but now you hear things differently.*

3. As you move on from this session, what practices might you adopt to keep the insights of this session alive in the way you engage with others, especially those closest to you?

4. Having met Barbara Cawthorne Crafton on DVD, you might be curious to know more about her ministry and to subscribe to *The Almost Daily eMos*. Go to http://www.geraniumfarm.org/home.cfm for more information on Barbara and The Geranium Farm.

Do you want freedom enough to turn your focus
from the one who hurt you to you, yourself, so that
you can...get out of jail..., a jail whose door you
continue to keep locked?

—Barbara Cawthorne Crafton

# SESSION | 3

## CHIPPING AWAY

### BEFORE THE SESSION

Many participants like to come to the group conversation after considering individually some of the issues that will be raised. The following five reflective activities are intended to open your mind, memories and emotions regarding some aspects of this session's topic. Use the space provided here to note your reflections.

1. What stories do you know around the theme of forgiveness—either forgiveness granted or forgiveness withheld? What insight have you gained from these stories?

2. In the first option, *The Story of Mrs. Lee and Mrs. Day* (p. 45), there are five statements from Barbara that give you a sense of the core of her teaching here. Where do these statements connect with your own experience of the power of forgiveness?

3. The third option, *Community Matters* (p. 49), recalls the events of October 2006, when a gunman shot children in an Amish school in Pennsylvania. You might wish to refresh your memory of that terrible event by going to some of the media reports of it and confronting once again your feelings both about the event and about the actions of the members of the Amish community.

4. The fourth option, *If You Forgive…*, offers a brief study in the Gospel of John. Take time prior to the group meeting to sit with the passage and allow it to inform your preparation for this session.

5. This week, where in your life, your community or our world have you noticed the power of forgiving—and not forgiving—? Where have you seen opportunities missed?

Included in this session is reflection on the place of community in the project of forgiveness. You will experience an emotional stretch all the way from a powerful story of Mrs. Lee and Mrs. Day, who lived in a congregation for years unable to get beyond their frozen unforgiving, to the memory of an Amish community that couldn't rest until forgiveness had been granted. In both cases the faith community played a key role in the lives of the individual members.

What would you say that this faith community means to you as an individual member of the congregation? How has it shaped you? In what ways does it continue to give meaning to your way of being in relationship?

Before selecting from the options that follow as a guide and catalyst for conversation, together watch *the entire portion of the DVD for Session 3*.

## OPTION 1: THE STORY OF MRS. LEE AND MRS. DAY

You have now experienced Barbara's gifts as storyteller as you listened to the story of Mrs. Lee and Mrs. Day. Having enjoyed the story, we will harvest the learnings from it. Here are five quotes from Barbara that will guide us in appreciating her reasons for telling this particular story:

*The thing we are focused on when we have been injured gives the perpetrator more power than he or she really has. When we turn and face the situation more accurately, he or she shrinks to a normal human size.*

*If the perpetrator does the deed and you hold on to the deed, you've helped the perpetrator continue the deed; you've become a co-conspirator with your own aggressor, not in a matter of guilt—the guilt is still theirs—but in the effect. There is a perverse identity between perpetrator and victim.*

*We can define ourselves as "the ones against so-and-so"; as the ones that must disagree with our enemy. Politics is often like that: "Well, I'm against whatever he's for." It becomes a substitute for thinking. We need to define ourselves as ourselves and not allow our enemy to define us.*

*Forgiveness is not this "wonderful thing" I'm going to do to welcome the perpetrator back into my world. Forgiveness is almost an act of self-love. It is a gift to myself. It is primarily for me that I need to forgive.*

*Do you want freedom enough to turn your focus from the one who has hurt you to*

*you, yourself, so that you alone can take the action you need to get out of jail—a jail the perpetrator may have built for you, but a jail whose door you continue to keep locked?*

1. What insights will you take from the story of Mrs. Lee and Mrs. Day and from Barbara's reflection about those two people and the choices they made?

2. When have you found yourself in the kind of relational jail that Barbara describes in the story and in her reflection? If you are still in one of those situations where you have given the perpetrator more power than is good for either of you, what options do you have to move on?

3. What options did the congregation of Mrs. Lee and Mrs. Day have other than building their own congregational life around the stubborn willfulness of these two "grand dames" of the congregation?

# OPTION 2: GLOBAL IMPLICATIONS

Barbara leads us on to see that the behavior of Mrs. Lee and Mrs. Day is visible in the choices we make as political communities and nation states.

People die from our identification of an enemy as the evil and our inability to see our own role in perpetuating international violence. Wars have never brought peace. Non-violence has brought peace.

The willingness to say, "Yes, so-and-so has done this to me, and it was bad; but I am not going to play, not going to do it back." What you do is stand. What you don't do is shoot back.

As nations, we most often choose war as our response to real or perceived violence against our people and borders. We join the perpetrators in their violence. We became makers of war. We think war will bring peace, but it doesn't. The world grows more dangerous because we choose war instead of some other action that would have been met with a different response.

1. From the vantage point of time, we look back over history, see through the violence of warfare and identify the implications of our national and international choices. Yet why is violence so often our response?

2. How do you grow a community or a nation that will choose an alternative to "joining the perpetrator"?

3. What role could forgiveness have played in the events, say, of 9/11? What role did forgiveness play? What role could forgiveness *still* play?

# OPTION 3: COMMUNITY MATTERS

Part of the response to questions raised in the Option 2 is in the example of a shooting in an Amish community in Pennsylvania in 2006.

Toni opens the discussion by wondering about the choices that a community makes when there is conflict. How does the community involve itself? What does the community do?

Barbara responds by drawing our attention to the shooting in October 2006 at the one-room Amish schoolhouse in Nickel Mines, Pennsylvania, when a gunman shot 10 girls, killing five of them, before shooting himself. Members of the Amish community comforted the gunman's family after the shooting and immediately extended forgiveness to the one who had brought such pain into their lives.

These Amish had been raised thinking of forgiveness so they knew that's what they had to do. They did it the next day. They could not be who they were unless they did this. They were horribly injured by the loss of their children, but they couldn't allow themselves to be further injured by not being who they were. Then they would have lost everything—not only their children, but themselves as will. The healing from this is still going on, but they made the first steps: walking down the road. They had each other and they had the teaching of their community. The world looked on and was amazed.

1. When have you experienced the power and values of a community to move individuals beyond thoughts of any response other than forgiveness?

2. What practices do you have in place in your congregation that could support you in making healthy responses to conflict both within your congregation and beyond it?

3. Following the shooting the West Nickel Mines School was torn down, and a new one-room schoolhouse, the New Hope School, was built at another location.

# OPTION 4: IF YOU FORGIVE...

Read this passage from the Gospel of John and the two reflections that follow:

John 20:19-23 *(NRSV)*

> When it was evening on that day, the first day of the week, and the doors of the house where the disciples had met were locked for fear of the Jews, Jesus came and stood among them and said, "Peace be with you." After he said this, he showed them his hands and his side. Then the disciples rejoiced when they saw the Lord. Jesus said to them again, "Peace be with you. As the Father has sent me, so I send you." When he had said this, he breathed on them and said to them, "Receive the Holy Spirit. If you forgive the sins of any, they are forgiven them; if you retain the sins of any, they are retained."

George reflects on this passage:

> *It's always been striking to me that he says to the disciples, "You have the power to forgive or to not forgive." It's a choice. This is a peak of our story and one to take with us. Somehow we can create community through this power to forgive. There's an implication that we may not, and we are free not to.*

Barbara reflects on this passage:

> *If you forgive the sins of any they are forgiven. If you welcome that person back into your community, they are in. It arises from within you. If you forgive that person, he or she is forgiven and enclosed again in the circle of who you are. That's not a statement about admission to heaven, but a statement about the inclusion, the admission into the community—the re-welcoming into the community.*
>
> *We think that we have the keys to forgiveness, and if one of the apostles forgives you, you get to go to heaven; if he doesn't, too bad for you! But I don't think it's about that. I think it's actually about the community. If we forgive the sins of any, they are forgiven. It means they are with us again. They are back. We know people left. People were at odds—left and didn't come back. All kinds of things have happened, but the community had the power to re-create itself out of the grace of forgiveness.*

1. What is your reading of this passage from the Gospel of John?

2. What light does this passage and your reflections throw on the life of your faith community? What practices of forgiveness might you adopt as a community that would draw you all into a deeper relationship with one another and with the Holy Spirt?

# OPTION 6: CLOSING PRAYER

Gracious God,
it is not always easy for us to understand ourselves,
let alone to understand you.
Sometimes we perceive things
in ways other than they really are.
Our emotions sometimes clouds our understanding.
Our wounds immobilize us.
Set us free to move into our future with you beside us
to show us the way forward,
and give us the courage to find a new path,
through Jesus Christ our Lord,
*Amen.*

Barbara Cawthorne Crafton, 2014

# OPTION 6: PERSONAL REFLECTION

## (for use following the session)

Following the session you will continue to think about issues raised both on the DVD and in your small group. This suggestion for journaling is offered to support you in continuing your reflection beyond the session time.

1. You may not have had time to complete all the options in the group study time. As you have time, take the opportunity for personal reflection on the ones that you missed, or the ones that were really engaging and to which you now want to return on your own.

2. Take time to reflect (and perhaps journal) on how the input and conversation has changed your attitude toward forgiveness. Remember how Barbara began her teaching in this session: "We think forgiveness is primarily about the perpetrator. Forgiveness is not as much about the perpetrator as it is about me. I am the one who carries it." Notice how this theme has run through the session and how it sits with you now.

3. In the opening of Session 2 you complete this statement, "Forgiveness is _____." How would you complete the statement now? in the same way or differently?

4. As you move on from this session, what practices might you adopt to keep the insights of this session alive in the way you engage with others, especially those closest to you?

5. Having met Barbara Cawthorne Crafton
   on DVD, you might be curious to know
   more about her ministry and to subscribe
   to *The Almost Daily eMos*. Go to http://
   www.geraniumfarm.org/home.cfm for more
   information on Barbara and The Geranium
   Farm.

In these intractable times where forgiveness seems impossible, step back and let God do some work. The sufficiency of God is bigger than ours.

—Barbara Cawthorne Crafton

# SESSION | 4

## HOW TO START

### BEFORE THE SESSION

Many participants like to come to the group conversation after considering individually some of the issues that will be raised. The following five reflective activities are intended to open your mind, memories and emotions regarding some aspects of this session's topic. Use the space provided here to note your reflections.

1. You are going to hear Barbara talking about prayer in this way: "Prayer is energy; prayer can flow through an opening which you create with just one word; prayer allows the strength and power of the universe to move through us if we allow it; and we can get into this river of life and love and go with it." How do you talk about prayer? What prayer practices have you found to be helpful in the project of rebuilding broken relationships?

2. In the course of this session you will hear Barbara speaking about shame and repentance. (See the notes for the second option, *Moving from Shame to Repentance*, p. 65.) In anticipation of this conversation, think about times when you have felt shame, as well as times when you have experienced the path of repentance and restoration of relationship. You might find it helpful to journal about these experiences prior to the session.

3. What concrete practices of forgiving and being forgiven have you found to be effective for you? (In the third option, *Three Concrete Physical Practices* [p. 67], you will find them mentioned; they will be described more fully in the session.)

4. During our lives we have had the opportunity to witness powerful acts of truth telling and reconciliation. Some of these are mentioned in the fifth option, *Witness to the Power of Reconciliation* (p. 71). In anticipation of this group conversation, you might look into the history of one of these national processes that drew international attention.

5. Include the *Closing Prayer* for this session (p. 72) in your prayer time this week. Reflect on the prayer in the space below. How is God answering your prayer?

You are about to hear Barbara speaking about the power of saying nothing more than the name of the person with whom you might be in a broken relationship.

As you come together in this fourth session of the series, take a moment to acknowledge the presence of each person in the group by going around the circle and simply saying together the name of each person. Take your time, allowing yourselves an opportunity to "see" the person even as you say their name.

Before selecting from the options that follow as a guide and catalyst for conversation, together watch the *entire portion of the DVD for Session 4*.

## OPTION 1: JUST SAY THE NAME, "JOE"

A powerful thread running through Barbara's teaching in this session emerges from the story of Joe and Erwin, the two evening prayer officiants in one of Barbara's parishes. You have heard the story of how Joe became a spiritual allergen for Erwin. And you have heard how Barbara provided Erwin with a kind of 'homeopathic cure' for this spiritual allergy in the form of a tiny prayer: Just say his name, "Joe."

Barbara offers a thoughtful progression of insight as she opens for us this concrete way of getting started on our forgiveness projects:

> *Putting a tiny bit of the offensive substance into the system repeatedly, bit by bit, over times helps the swelling to go down. The swelling has to go down in order to get healed from the allergy itself.*

> *Using this prayer of the name means you can let God do the work. Don't you do the work.*

> *Over time you will change. This prayer will change you for sure. It will also change the one whose name it is.*

> *Prayer is energy. It's the gift of God's energy. Love is energy. We are made of God's energy and love.*

> *In saying the name, "Joe," you begin to create an opening through which this energy can flow.*

> *Over time you change. Something good will happen to the person you are praying for; the energy of God does not create evil.*

> *In these intractable situations where forgiveness seems impossible, step back and let God do some work. The sufficiency of God is bigger than ours.*

> *It involves not trying to run everything ourselves, not thinking that forgiveness is a job we need to do. All we have to do—like all the spiritual practices—is to ask for it.*

> *You say the name and you allow God to do the healing. You are patient with it.*

> *You expect a miracle but you don't know what it is because prayer isn't shaping; we don't order stuff and send it back if it's not what we want.*

> *It is just coming into the presence of God and allowing ourselves to be open channels for the love of God.*

1. What are your "Joe" stories where you might have responded to a "spiritual allergy" through something as simple as saying the name of the other as part of your regular prayer practice?

2. Barbara clearly has a way of "seeing" prayer: prayer is energy; prayer can flow through an opening which you create with just one word; prayer allows the strength and power of the universe to move through us if we allow it; and we can get into this river of life and love and go with it.

   • Where does Barbara's teaching on prayer practice intersect with your experience of prayer?

   • What new possibilities of prayer are opened in you as you listen to Barbara?

# OPTION 2: MOVING FROM SHAME TO REPENTANCE

Barbara gently but firmly accompanies us along the path from shame to repentance and leads us into a simple practice of visualization and gesture that can be very potent in the journey from shame to forgiveness:

> I tend to continue to feel ashamed or mad about something long ago and then it bursts into flame. Shame is like that. Shame can't speak. Shame is mute.
>
> A way to begin to get on the other side is to face the shame and speak it. Repentance can speak. Repentance can say: I did this and I wish I hadn't. I am sorry.
>
> Shame can't do any of that. Shame is terrified of being found out and so shame hides. In shame we carry the sins of others, and our own sins, close to us. We can't let go of them. We won't let go of them. I just want to keep it quiet.
>
> If I'm in shame and I can't speak it, how can it get better? How can I have light if I'm terrified of the light? How can I speak, if I'm afraid to speak?
>
> The sooner we get from shame to repentance, the better; there's something we can do about it.
>
> In the silence of your life, there is one to whom you can speak. It is God. If you have no words, then offer it to God as an image…

Barbara illustrates the practice like this:

> Picture yourself as the child you once were. There was a time before any of this happened. We come into this world innocent. Picture that child on the hand of God.

> Up to now that child has been lodged inside, hiding away in your heart.
>
> Take your young self out from inside and hold her here. Do it with your hand: here she was hiding; and now she is here. Look at that child. Imagine the love of God pouring on her, on him…

1. Where does this path from shame to repentance feel familiar to you?

2. Are you able to identify in the safety of this group a situation that you want to transform in some way where you see that Barbara's teaching could be helpful for you? What is that?

# OPTION 3: THREE CONCRETE PHYSICAL PRACTICES

Barbara has introduced us to three specific physical practices that will physically and spiritually remind us of who we are:

- *Prayer of Name Only*: Picture yourself walking away when you use the prayer of the name alone, allowing God to do the healing in the space you have opened with the name.
- *Be-holding Yourself*: Take yourself from your heart and hold yourself out at arm's length, seeing yourself the way God sees you.
- *Shower of Love*: Whenever you take a shower, let the water pour on you in a gracious, lovely, cleansing stream and remember that this is the way God loves you.

Patrice speaks of a practice she has followed of writing the name of person she cannot bring herself to speak with on a piece of paper and placing that paper between the pages of a psalm and leaving it there. "I've found that my seeing their name there changes my attitude toward them."

1. You see the intent of these practices. Which of them might you take on and include in your spiritual practices?

2. What other practices might support you in
   your desire to address issues of forgiveness,
   shame, and repentance?

# OPTION 4: TO FORGIVE OR NOT TO FORGIVE

Tapua speaks about the pleasure that can derive from revenge and not forgiving:

> *What can be challenging sometimes is that I don't want to forgive this person until they get their just deserts; until I see them fall or fail. You deny me that if I let them off the hook. They need to get fixed first, and then I can consider forgiving them.*

In response Barbara looks at the situation from both sides—the forgiver and the forgiven—and leads us to look at the sweet freedom that lies beyond the unwillingness to forgive and be forgiven:

> *Forgiveness is about me and my freedom ("You may or may not be sorry, but if you're not I forgive you anyway.")*
>
> *It's up to you who you forgive; it's not up to the other.*
>
> *If he can't be sorry it's true that he can't experience your forgiveness—he won't know the sweetness of it—he'll still be back in his vendetta, but you won't. You'll be free.*
>
> *We have lots of opportunities to forgive that don't depend on the feelings of others or even our own feelings.*

1. How might you get beyond that feeling that Tapua describes—that sense of wanting revenge and wanting to see the other "fixed" so that they earn your forgiveness? What is there in Barbara's teaching that opens up other options for you?

2. Clearly there are choices for both the perpetrator who needs forgiveness and for the victim who has the power to forgive. What personal situations have deepened your humanity and your wisdom in this matter of the choice to forgive or not to forgive?

# OPTION 5: WITNESS TO THE POWER OF RECONCILIATION

During our lives we have had the opportunity to witness powerful acts of truth-telling and reconciliation. Some of these will be very familiar to the members of your group. Here are three prominent examples with which you are likely familiar and which might prompt you to think of others:

• The Truth and Reconciliation Commission of South Africa, beginning in 1996

• National Unity and Reconciliation Commission of Rwanda, established in 1999 (The New York Times of April 5, 2014 featured photographic portraits by Pieter Hugo of genocidal victims and perpetrators together 20 years after the time in Rwanda when a million people were killed during that country's genocide. This gallery of pictures is a remarkable testimony to the possibility of reconciliation even in the most horrendous situations.)

• The Truth and Reconciliation Commission of Canada which expressed its purpose in this way:

> There is an emerging and compelling desire to put the events of the past behind us so that we can work towards a stronger and healthier future. The truth telling and reconciliation process as part of an overall holistic and comprehensive response to the Indian Residential School legacy is a sincere indication and acknowledgement of the injustices and harms experienced by Aboriginal people and the need for continued healing. This is a profound commitment to establishing new relationships embedded in mutual recognition and respect that will forge

> a brighter future. The truth of our common experiences will help set our spirits free and pave the way to reconciliation.

1. What experiences have members of the group had in relation to this international movement toward truth-telling as a path of reconciliation?

2. Restorative Justice is another expression of this larger movement that attempts to open up spaces of truth, healing, justice and freedom for both perpetrators and victims. What insights do members of the group have about this approach to restoration and justice?

# OPTION 6: CLOSING PRAYER

O God, help us to turn to you as a first step,
not as a last resort.
Where our prayer fails to calm our troubled souls,
show us the prayer that will,
for yours is the power we need
in order to forgive and reclaim the life you desire for us,
God of our strength and God of our peace,
*Amen.*

*Barbara Cawthorne Crafton, 2014*

# OPTION 7: PERSONAL REFLECTION

### (for use following the session)

Following the session you will continue to think about issues raised both on the DVD and in your small group. This suggestion for journaling is offered to support you in continuing your reflection beyond the session time.

1. You may not have had time to complete all the options in the group study time. As you have time, take the opportunity for personal reflection on the ones that you missed, or the ones that were really engaging and to which you now want to return on your own.

2. As you move on from this session, find a way to maintain your awareness of the practices that were introduced in the third option on page 67, especially 'The Shower of Love."

3. Some of the powerful acts of truth telling and reconciliation mentioned in the fifth option, *Witness to the Power of Reconciliation* (p. 71), may have piqued you interest. Consider looking into the history of one of these national processes that drew such massive international attention.

4. Having met Barbara Cawthorne Crafton on DVD, you might be curious to know more about her ministry and to subscribe to *The Almost Daily eMos*. Go to http://www.geraniumfarm.org/home.cfm for more information on Barbara and The Geranium Farm.

When we refuse to forgive, we shrink our world. It is against God's reality for us to shrink the world...

—Barbara Cawthorne Crafton

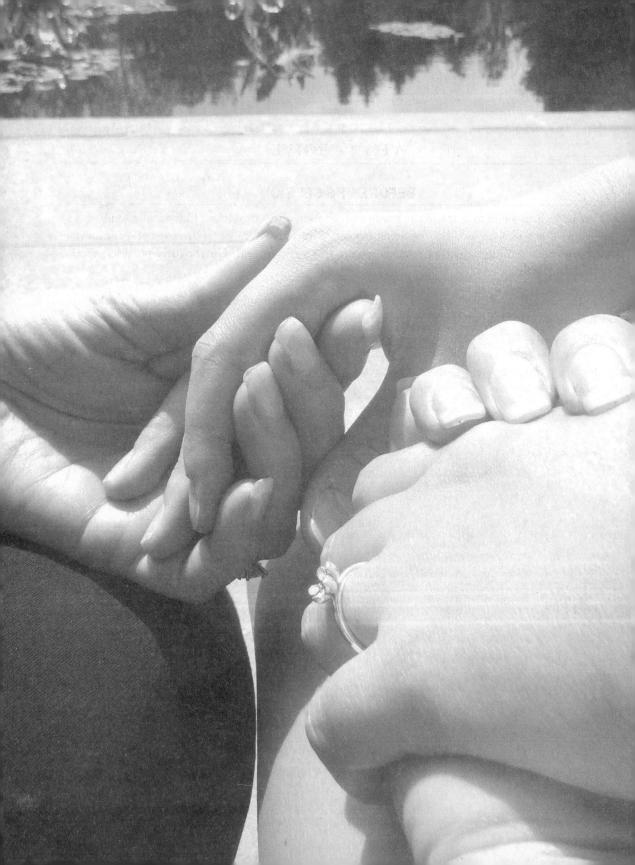

# SESSION | 5

## WHY FORGIVE?

### BEFORE THE SESSION

Many participants like to come to the group conversation after considering individually some of the issues that will be raised. The following five reflective activities are intended to open your mind, memories and emotions regarding some aspects of this session's topic. Use the space provided here to note your reflections.

1. In the first option, *Going with the Flow* (p. 81), you will see 10 points that summarize Barbara's theological case for forgiveness. If you have been participating in the series to this point, these will not be surprising to you; they concisely summarize Barbara's teaching on God, Creation, Love and Forgiveness, which we have been following during the four previous sessions. The question is "Why forgive?" This response is Barbara's bottom line, so to speak. What is your best and deepest response to that question? Take time to think about this and to write if you are so inclined.

2. Sit with the 16 statements of principle offered in the second option, *Living in the Way of Love and Forgiveness* (p. 82). Highlight the ones that speak most clearly to you. Think about which ones offer the most challenge for you in your life and relationship with God right now.

3. In anticipation of Barbara's teaching on the theme, "Why Forgive?" recall situations where you have forgiven someone and what it was that motivated you. Why did you forgive? What was the outcome for you and for the other? Reading Toni's description in the third option, *Knowing What to Embrace* (p. 83), provides a model for this kind of remembering.

4. Take time to review the topics and notes from the previous four sessions so that you have a clearer sense of the totality of this program—what you have learned, how you have grown in awareness. This will prepare you for the group sharing in the fourth option, *Closing Reflections* (p. 84).

5. Use the closing prayers from the five sessions in your personal prayer time as a spiritual discipline and preparation for this final session.

In this final session make sure to leave time for these aspects of group closure:
- Wrap up whatever is unfinished.
- Express appreciation for the contributions each member has made.
- Hear the difference it has made for each person to participate (see #4: *Closing Reflections,* p. 84).
- Give thanks to God for the gifts, insights, relationships and sacred guidance of this time.
- Clean up your meeting space.

Before selecting from the options that follow as a guide and catalyst for conversation, together watch the *entire portion of the DVD for Session 5.*

## OPTIONS 1: GOING WITH THE FLOW

A friend told Barbara that if someone offends him, then that other person is essentially dead to him. This assertion leads Barbara into a compelling theological reflection which responds powerfully to the question, "Why forgive?" Here are 10 quotes from Barbara's case for forgiveness:

*If someone has to be dead to me, then the world I hold is maimed, it's damaged, it's not complete, and it's not true, because the person is not dead and does have lines in my play. I can't take a pencil and draw a line through that person's role in my life.*

*The power of God, the energy of God, is the energy of existence, not non-existence. God is about being, not non-being.*

*God is not a God who wants us to be less than we are. God is a God who has created us to be everything that we can be.*

*When we refuse to forgive, we shrink our world. It is against God's reality for us to shrink the world, because God's energy has created an expanding universe, not a shrinking one.*

*God has set into motion this energetic creation so that we would be seeking our union with God. God attracts and we respond.*

*There is a potent attractiveness between us and among us that is part of the attraction God has for us and the response we have toward God.*

*To stand back from forgiveness is to feel that you can somehow decide not to be attracted to God.*

*If my anger at you continues to sit in here (heart), I will be less able to respond authentically to the God who longs for me to respond.*

*Wouldn't it be better to have the energy of anger and non-forgiveness to use in some way other than keeping each other at arm's length?*

*The energy of God, the love of God flows unimpeded—a strong and powerful river. Wouldn't it be better to let that river flow without any of the dams that could interrupt the flow of it?*

Test the validity of these 10 statements for you by considering these kinds of questions:
- When have you felt "penciled out" of someone's world? What was that like?
- What happened on occasions when you were trying to shrink your world while God was working to expand it?
- What's that like when you just allow yourself to be drawn by the magnetic energy of God and let that be the force at work in your relationships?
- When have you noticed the difference between living fully into the spaciousness of God's creation as opposed to expending energy on anger and non-forgiveness?

# OPTION 2: LIVING IN THE WAY OF LOVE AND FORGIVENESS

Barbara's opening teaching also contains 16 principles that support living that is aligned with the flow of sacred energy. Here are some of these insights or principles:

1. The whole of humanity, no matter what any one individual has done to me, is included in my world.

2. Life is so precious and short that I will affirm the living reality of anyone who comes my way.

3. The world I hold is complete and true.

4. The power of God is the energy of existence, not non-existence.

5. Truth can exist even in the face of fear, pain and shame.

6. God has created us to be everything that we can be.

7. God has created an expanding universe. I will not shrink my world.

8. I hear the voices of all, whether they agree with me or not.

9. God has set into motion this energetic creation so that we would seek union with God.

10. There is a potent attraction between us that is part of the attraction God has for us.

11. When we pray for someone we are aligning ourselves to respond to the pull of God.

12. Being attracted to God means that I will be attracted to all God's people.

13. Forgiving is one way of participating in God's dance of life.

14. When I deal with my anger I am more able to respond authentically to God who longs for my response.

15. When I forgive I free up space and energy that can be used in some other way.

16. The energy and love of God will flow unimpeded like a powerful river if we allow it.

Which of these 16 principles attract you as you come to the end of this series of sessions on forgiveness? Get together with one or two others and talk about commitments that you might make in allowing some of these qualities to be more present in your practices and relationships.

In her closing reflection, Toni witnesses to her own capacity to move beyond the anger of betrayal and free up space and energy for a new time. In this reflection Toni is modeling what we talked about in the second option (p. 82)—allowing certain principles to inform her interactions with people who have hurt her and refusing to shrink her world.

> *There was a deep sense of betrayal. The anger in me was deep and strong. I'm standing, knowing that I have to be a sensible person on the surface. We have planned a farewell party for this person and this person comes and steps in front of me and says, "Toni, I'm going to miss you." I could not say honestly that I was going to miss this person, but something still happened. I was able to physically embrace that person and in that moment, somewhere in my brain I knew this was the beginning of a healing for me. (We both knew what the circumstances were. We both knew the truth.) The embrace wasn't just the physical embracing; it was embracing the idea that there is forgiveness and that I am at the beginning of forgiving the person who had betrayed me.*

> *I have appreciated this time of learning. I leave wondering about the practice I can do with things that aren't as deep as that betrayal, so that I can get that attraction again.*

What are you ready to embrace as a result of the insights you have harvested during these five session?

# OPTION 4: CLOSING REFLECTIONS

Following Toni's lead, each of the other participants offers a brief insight gleaned from the five sessions they have spent together:

Patrice:

> *We all want to be attracted to God's love and goodness. Part of forgiving is seeing that attraction in each other and being willing to allow ourselves to be drawn to it—allowing God to do that work.*

George:

> *When I strip away everything that forgiveness is not, it leaves a mysterious core at the center. This really is something that comes from God. It's something that I'm really dependent on God for. It leaves me with a sense of trust: being open to what God is going to do in forgiving, blessing, and bringing love into my life in the future as in the past. It's mysterious.*

Ryan:

> *The importance of creativity within forgiveness will be closer to my mind and heart. Sometimes we give up forgiving someone because we're frustrated and we might let it sit for a bit. But just as with creation, one can always work with it. If you are in the spirit of creation, the spirit of flexibility—living with the discomfort of that, you are able to grow, heal and become a new person.*

Tapua:

> *I'm thinking of how you value something when you've worked for it and paid for it. When I work to forgive somebody, it's easier for me to accept God's forgiveness of my sins. If I can take that shower (of God's blessing) every day and really believe that, no matter how bad it is, it has been forgiven, then I can truly believe that I have been forgiven. That's a wonderful way to wake up!*

Ralph:

> *I'm not sure I ever realized until today that there is more than one way to forgive. There is more than one road; it's unique for each person.*

Barbara:

> *Forgiveness is a decision made in the Spirit of God, a theological decision to claim freely in my present and my future, unencumbered by guilt from the past, accepting the promise of God that I am wiped clean and free.*

1. What insights did you each glean from the series?

2. What are you taking away from your participation in the life of this group that will make a difference for you in your ongoing pursuit of forgiveness?

# OPTION 5: CLOSING PRAYER

Loving God,
You do not withhold your love from us,
even when we withhold our love from one another and from you.
Help us to find the joy that comes
in shaping our lives to show forth your life in us.
Keep us mindful of Jesus' commandment
to love you and our neighbor fully.
In your own most holy Name we pray.
*Amen.*

*Barbara Cawthorne Crafton, 2014*

# OPTION 6: PERSONAL REFLECTION

## (for use following the session)

Following the session you will continue to think about issues raised both on the DVD and in your small group. This suggestion for journaling is offered to support you in continuing your reflection beyond the session time.

1. Make time to complete any of the program options that you didn't have time for during the session.

2. As you conclude this final session in the series of five, recall what you've learned from the other members of the group, what they chose to reveal of themselves, and what opened for each of them as a result of Richard's teaching. Hold members with gratitude, love and respect in a time of prayer and meditation.

3. Consider making a copy of the 16 principles that are listed in the second option, *Living in the Way of Love and Forgiveness* (p. 82), and placing them somewhere visible where they will remind you of some of the intentions you developed through your exposure to the teaching of Barbara Crafton.

4. Having met Barbara Cawthorne Crafton on DVD, you might be curious to know more about her ministry and to subscribe to *The Almost Daily eMos*. Go to http://www.geraniumfarm.org/home.cfm for more information on Barbara and The Geranium Farm.

# NOTES

# NOTES

# NOTES

# NOTES

# NOTES

# NOTES

# NOTES